Begin in Gladness

BEGIN IN GLADNESS

Michael Palma

STAR CLOUD PRESS
Scottsdale, Arizona

BEGIN IN GLADNESS
Michael Palma

cover design: Josh Levitas
cover photo: Michael Palma
author photo: Victoria Palma
back cover photo: Samuel Murray

Published by

~ STAR CLOUD PRESS ~ ~

6137 East Mescal Street
Scottsdale, Arizona 85254-5418

978-1-932842-58-6 — Paperback — $ 12.95

www.StarCloudPress.com

Library of Congress Control Number: 2011928864

Printed in the United States of America

Acknowledgments

Thanks are due to the editors of the following journals, in which some of the poems in this volume have previously appeared:

Café Review: "The Day," "Life and Times," "Light and Sweet," "Like Any Clown"; *Chelsea:* "Air of Lost Connections," "The Free Man"; *The Cornelian:* "Truth"; *Gradiva:* "A Band of Bards" (as "*IPSA Facta*"), "Serendipity" (with accompanying Italian translation by Luigi Fontanella); *Iambs & Trochees:* "Memorabilia," "Portrait with Mirrors," "When in April"; *Italian Americana:* "'Oh to Break Through,'" "Requiem for a Practical Possum"; *Pivot:* "Burlesque"; *Raintown Review:* "Figures of Frost"; *Shakespeare Newsletter:* "A Suit of Sables"; *Si Scrive:* "Multitudes" (with accompanying Italian translation by Luigi Fontanella).

"Dark and Deeper" appeared in *A Tumult for John Berryman,* edited by Marguerite Harris.

"Burlesque" was reprinted in *A Carrellata of Poets,* edited by Masja Dingjan and Paolo Valesio.

"Requiem for a Practical Possum" was reprinted in *Wild Dreams: The Best of Italian Americana,* edited by Carol Bonomo Albright and Joanna Clapps Herman.

"Air of Lost Connections" (with accompanying Italian translation by Alessandro Carrera) was reprinted in *Binding the Lands: Present Day Poets, Present Day Poetry,* edited by Alessandro Carrera and Alessandro Vettori.

"When in April," "Portrait with Mirrors," "The Ghost of Congress Street," "'Oh to Break Through'" and "Air of Lost Connections" appeared online in *The Ghost of Congress Street: New and Selected Poems.*

For MARY *and* DANA GIOIA,
who know what matters.

Contents

4

5

We Poets in our youth begin in gladness;
But thereof come in the end despondency and madness.

—Wordsworth

Do I contradict myself?
Very well then I contradict myself,
(I am large, I contain multitudes.)

—Whitman

Hypocrite Lecteur

Look through my eyes,
A streaked pane.
Try my brain
In your head for size.

Wriggle your hands
In mine like gloves.
Everyone loves
To take a chance.

Have some fun.
Go on, it's free.
No one will see,
And no harm done.

Your secret's hid
With me forever.
You know I'll never
Tell what we did.

1

When in April

In memory of Nolan Fallahay

There was a teacher of the company
Who make up the fat world, and such was he
That I was always glad to take my seat
Among the young who gathered at his feet,
For he was often merry in his prime
And fed us well on argument and rhyme.
He'd never bow his head at Shakespeare's name,
But lit instead a Canterbury flame.
"Quem quaeritis?" came from his lips each day,
Then "What is the young man trying to say?"
Would follow, and if any dared reply,
"What else?" he'd roar, so none could bull him by.
When someone spoke, no matter on what note,
He had some turned remark that he could quote,
And what was the connection, none could tell,
But all agreed he said it very well.
His clothing stopped in 1944,
His reading several centuries before.
With hawklike nose, a frame erect and thin,
A cigarette as constant as his chin,
All angles, and his hair the merest fuzz,
A Sherlock Holmes with a crewcut he was.
He would regale us ever and again
By speaking mockingly of famous men,

Or say, while smiling sweetly as a flower,
"As I once said to General Eisenhower...."
In God's good words he always did believe,
But wore it in his work, not on his sleeve.
An honest man in a dishonest age,
He saved his blackest bile and loudest rage
For all those foolish bastards who insist
Their reeking nether regions must be kissed.
The world revolved, he followed his career,
And fewer sat before him every year.
He could not go the way that others went
But clung to what he'd dreamed was permanent
Till he, who had so happily begun,
Was glad as any when his course was done.
He left his stage, and left behind a name
That carried less and less to those who came
To clog the corridors where he had walked.
In rooms that once vibrated when he talked
I still can see him curling round his book,
Laughing at God knows what until he shook,
Coughing and choking till he had to sit,
As folly danced much faster than his wit.

A Suit of Sables

"Nay, then, let the devil wear black, for I'll have a suit of sables."

Encountering Hamlet after twenty years,
Long years of pirouette and perigee,
With flesh more sullied and more solid now
Than ever dreamt in my philosophy,
I pass, and watch the flecked procession pass,
The mumming player strutting as he goes,
The plate of fashion and the horse of clothes,
The rings and rays of hairburst that enclose
The twisting mouth-hole and the thrusting nose.
How stale, flat, and unprofitable appears
This muddy frolic to the indifferent eye,
This rout of bung-hole stoppers, and yet how
I save my fiercest grin for when I spy
This final mincing monster in the glass.

The Day

1/14/71

I always made an awkward bow.
God bless you! And God bless
John Keats who died
Today in Rome,
Twenty-five years, one hundred
And fifteen days old.
The lungs were
Completely gone.
The doctors could not imagine
How he had lived
In the last two months.

Poetry had died first,
As slow a death.
Today I am old as Keats,
Twenty-five years, one hundred
And fifteen days, enough
For a poet, *for it runs*
In my head we shall all die
Young. My breathless poems
Surround me, my days run on
Like water,
I've missed my chance.

I feel the flowers growing
Over me. And bless
John Keats who died
Choking on his sweetness.
Tomorrow I shall be
Older than Keats,
Dreaming in the morning
Of the traces
Of fresh dark blood
All over the bed,
Blood to make new poems from.

A Magic Lantern

My image of my thirties already shows
A fading face, a lumbering form. I glower
Dimly at distant shores that no one knows.
Father broods overhead in his shabby coat.
Melody bubbles from my aching throat,
I pluck the music of the decaying hour.

Hallam is dead, is dead. Such hope I had,
All dead with him. I burrowed for relief
But voices murmured, poets must be sad,
It is the call. I mourned for years and years,
Gorging on the rich red meat of grief,
Bathing in my calcifying tears.

Life like a favorite novel went on and on.
They know not me. I am become a book.
I gathered praise like pins, I prowled the lawn
Like a dirty monk, I saw the faces poke
Through hedges for a touch, a word, a look.
Bent with the stars, I went inside to smoke.

Beloved Lincolnshire uphold my feet,
Save me oh save me who can hardly stand.
My Sovereign rides astride the breaking sea,
Come to the window, see the British fleet
Sink down into the garden. Lord, how grand.
This world. This flesh. This garden. Gather me.

A roll of muffled drums. Slowly they bring
The graven figure heavy with the word,
Easing me downward, sealing me with night,
Casing me in a blunt box, binding me tight,
Stamping me deep. And still the voices sing
With harmonies the children never heard.

Memorabilia

I have seen glory twice, when all is told.
The first was when a woman came to me,
Her hair unbound and sprinkled with the rain.
Sun on my pillow dried it tenderly.

The other time? If memory will allow,
Something about a poet I saw plain,
Who stopped and spoke to me, but I am old
And find it hard recalling such things now.

The Choice

The intellect of man is forced to choose
Perfection of the life, or of the work,
And if it take the second must refuse
A heavenly mansion, raging in the dark.
                                —W. B. Yeats

Perfection of the life's a thoughtless quest,
The vain hope of the vain. You sought this first,
Embraced assurances to save your soul,
Then sat and watched them wither in the night.
Perfection of the work gave more control,
Or so it promised to the mind athirst
For what might calm the churning of the breast.
You raged in darkness and you raged in light,
Gibed at the fools in boulevards, and cursed
The jagged parts that failed to make the whole.
Then, flinching from the arrogance of the worst,
You poised yourself amid antinomies,
Speaking most truly when you spoke of these,
Knowing that knowing least is knowing best.

The intellect inhabits the absurd.
Men choose between impossibilities
And every answer is an empty one,
Whether composed of words or of the Word.
The creeds and cantos interleave to say
That we must grind and suffer, either way.

13

Your singing currents tell us, as they run
Around the stone in the middle of the stream,
That sandy pillars are to be preferred
To none at all, that we must strive to seize
An immortality that lasts a day,
And hearts are wise that will not be deterred
From airy hopes and love that is a dream,
Where pain is solid and has come to stay.

The Free Man

In the prison of his days
Teach the free man how to praise.
                    —W. H. Auden

When Europe was a disease,
Conscience like cosmetics
Coated the face
Sculpted from clear ice.

Tapered fingers fondling
Each cigarette,
His gestures hardened
Into our dogmas.

Omnivorous for mountains,
Devouring rivers,
Maven of maps,
He swallowed the world.

Face grown forward
And seamed like a fjord,
He did as he pleased,
He formed himself.

Who can ever be contained
    In someone's need to show
The chairs right-angled to the wall,
    The books all in a row?

And who has never felt the prick,
    On which so much depends,
To thrust a fat tongue out just as
    The shutter blade descends?

Nine hundred pages (many flat,
No one can win so much as that)
Of *sprezzatura, sprachgefühl,*
Of wrestling the ineffable,
Instinct with every style and mood,
With every form and attitude
From public robe to seminude,
Bright with the burden of his gift,
His words still make us want to lift
The telephone to cry bravo,
Certain he would have liked to know.

16

When violence was a virtue,
When yelpers and yahoos roamed
Uprooting borders boldly,
He was gentlest of men, least vicious.
This too should be recalled.

From trampolines of tongue
When he was young

To carpet-slipper measures
Of age's pleasures,

In our sky lingers
A blur of nimble fingers,

In the long night
An arabesque of light.

So prodigious his blessings, all but
The least of his leavings would be
The making of many lessers.

He died in early autumn, promptly shrunken
To low predictions in the morning paper
Of his coming insignificance, misreadings
Of the vivid blood still pulsing through the corpus
And the shadow thrown across the mind forever.
The man of culture shuffles through his castle,
Whose walls are mortared with the blood of millions.
He cannot stop their dying. He can work puzzles,
He can erect umbrellas of understanding
(One page of hell worth more than whether Dante
Was Ghibelline or Guelph, or why they battled)
And respect what mocks at understanding, knowing
Bad verse especially makes nothing happen.
Loud sonnets fill no bellies, and machine-guns
Trained mercilessly upon the inconvenient
Are never stopped by odes appropriating
The clean souls of the victims, fixing evil
Forever in the other. In the real morning
Car radios tell us of the floods in China
Killing ten thousand, and we fret all evening
Over the tapping noise inside the engine.
No man is not an island. The true battle
Is always inward, the turn aside from loving.
His pleasures pleasant as his muse grew modest,
He studied both the mirror and the window.
He wore our human skin, and sought our pardon
For telling us the truth of what we are.

*

Through all, he honored us
By wearing the helplessness
Of being one of us.

He vivified our ground
With the currents of his mind.
Let the tall harvest stand.

Across cold seas he came
To conscience, his true home.
He honored the word. Honor him.

2

Burlesque

The curtain opens and the poem comes out
In checkered suspenders and a funny hat,
Grinning and mugging across the sanded stage.
Tatata tatata tatata raa
Says the pumping orchestra. The poem says,
"Hiya folks, these are the jokes."

"Blaaaugh! What crap! Get off the stage!"
Pelting from the galleries with fat fruit.
The penny-seaters toss their programs away
And clamor for the spirit of the age:
"A poem should be palpable and mute!"
Okay.

Another poem comes out and does a strip,
Peeling off adjectives with sensual jerks.
The orchestra gets too caught up to work.
The poem struts its pink-tipped verbs
And tosses its final image into the crowd:
"How'm I doin', Ezra?" The place goes wild.

The emcee hops up to the mike:
"You always pay for what you like!"
He closes the show to cheering, reading
From a card: "Portions of the preceding
Program hang out in a tent on Dover Beach
With anyone whose grasp exceeds his reach."

Views from a Summer Vacation

(Reading Berryman in isolation)

His head hurts from doing no work,
From living on sandwiches,
And from carrying solid blocks of it
Inside him all the day.

His skull feels two sizes too tight.
How can he feel this way
When he doesn't even drink?
Believe me, friends, it's not easy.

Soon his head will hurt again
When he stands before students,
Thrashing in a holy fit,
Sweat coating his lank serpent.

The unreflecting mirrors of their faces
Will turn to one another, saying
This must be something, whatever it is,
Too bad there isn't any use for it.

And never in all these years,
In all those faces,
Will he make out a flicker. But it's all right.
Climb in beside me, Muse, and hold on tight.

Portrait with Mirrors

The expense of spirit in a waste of shame
Is my pursuit, now I have lost the name
Of action, and must trace how I became
A shadow man, a thing of tags and patches
Carving the classics into snack-sized snatches,
Rictus rigidifying as he watches
The young ones splash in the genetic pool,
It's who I am the one and only rule
Of life or art these days, when any fool
May look into his heart and write, it seems.
I have wept at the uncoupling of my dreams.
I have measured out my life with freshman themes.

In the House of Messer Violi

Phrases tossed like custard pies,
Cascading intellect,
And the size
Of a flagrant but well-groomed
Imagination
That lit up every poem
Signaled what to expect,
Or at least what we assumed,
When we had an invitation
To dinner at his home.

Driving down a lane
That wriggled through big woods
And little neighborhoods
Brought the first flutters
Of something amiss.
Houses spotted the terrain.
None were red with orange shutters,
None were green with purple shutters,
None had striped or dotted gutters,
Not even his.

He led us inside,
Stained from suburban labors
Like his neighbors,
And displayed with pride

A wife who radiated grace
From a symmetrical face,
Who invited us to take
Not moth-lips or flamingo pies
Garnished with something's eyes,
But sizzling patriotic steak.

After dinner we sat waiting
For him to climb
The table and start gyrating,
An out-of-body bard
Keening in multilingual rhyme.
In the dark yard
His cigarette tips glowed
As his effortlessly brainy,
Relentlessly unzany
Conversation flowed.

Tucked into our car once more,
We rolled through woods
In a delighted daze,
Spiraling past the platitudes
Of our imagining to place
A merry Beckett on a shore
Of cold moonlit beauty
Writing tortured plays
Purely out of duty
To a groaning and bewildered race.

Multitudes

He is darling, he is daddy,
He is doctor and professor
And mower of the lawn.
In the market in his sweater
He smiles among the soup.
Charity ladies linger
In the doorway, enjoying his pipe.

Smelly with colored hair
He chases the cheerleaders,
Craving their tight little asses.
His scars glow in the dark,
He crawls across the desk,
He croons to himself. Two fingers
Are gone from his right foot.

Finally the lines are tight,
Toward dawn the poem lies
Drenched and flecked with foam,
The newest thing in the world.
Shrunken in his sweater,
Humming, he sidles crabwise
Up the stairs to bed.

Life and Times

In youth he struck off quick pointillist poems.
In no time they were rendered into French.
He sat vivid at his desk and said *I'll show 'em.*
Bouncing shopgirls read him marvelous with lunch.
Pontiffs were benign. Posterity was a cinch.

He tried growing older. The lines tried growing longer.
Now some were thick and sometimes some were flat.
Nobody nowadays called him the wizard singer,
But he had gnarled wisdom. Nothing wrong with that.
In guarded benevolence the old gods sat.

The works collected, too much for even lawyers.
He was named in respectable places instead of read.
Explainers were all parsing the new boyos.
The last book made no one believe he wasn't still dead.
He fashioned his final lines on his final bed.

Some saw the lips move, but none could make out what was said.

3

A Band of Bards

Does anyone remember when
The Italian poets came to town?
Like the Assyrian they came down,
Devouring the old streets, and then
Followed the signs that bade us come
To an airless auditorium.
The one with the bowtie and beard
Was first to speak, and it appeared
He was the boss man of the troupe.
His verses showed a tenderness
His face tried hard not to express.
The next one, tall enough to stoop,
Would flash a jack-o'-lantern smile,
All weariness and irony
In person, not in poetry.
His passion held us for a while.
Following him, a weathered one
Exuded seriousness like sweat.
His mouth embraced a cigarette
And poems full of myth and sun.
A quiet man in an old sweater
Wore his eyeglasses on a string.
His poems didn't care to sing,
Which made some people like them better.
Then one in black with silver hair
And dotted scarf around his throat

Threw down his poems like a dare,
Which some thought was the proper note.
A sad-faced and slope-shouldered man
Imposed on us with two or three
Slivers of sensitivity
That almost turned away and ran.
The next one read a sequence fraught
With Christian sensibility,
But before he could present it, he
Had to think about himself being caught
Thinking of what he thought he thought.
Then one with open shirt and face
Tried hard to show us how to find
A windswept, unforgiven place
In the green pages of his mind.
Another, solid and well dressed,
Immobile at the microphone,
Tolled in a rolling baritone
Poems of love, and no one guessed
He was as frightened as the rest.
Two women read, one short and strong
Who took command of every ear,
The other languid, thin and long.
She made us come to her to hear.
And nearly bringing up the rear
Appeared the second in command,
Who in a voice to conjure fear
Read poems filled with wind and sand
And sea and stars and child and cheer.

The last one was a kind of a star
Who sang and played on the guitar
Tart words and tender melodies,
A combination sure to please,
Till he announced he'd sing a song
That was a hundred stanzas long.
More poets took the podium
Than there were people who had come.
They smiled at all the empty seats
And seemed to get on very well,
Although for all we knew they might,
When they were on their own ground, fight
Like a cage of starving parakeets.
They nosed about the local scene
Until they found a swank hotel
Whose piano bar played *Gershaveen,*
And then their plane was in the air
As if they never had been there.
Yet I remember, all the same,
The day the Italian poets came.

La Vita Letteraria

1

Friday. Latina

An anonymous poet has inscribed the wall
Of a public building in letters two feet tall:
Roma campione, Lazio coglione.
At the cultural meeting, someone I haven't met
Hands me a typed paragraph in Italian
For me to ad lib into the microphone.
In my own extempore speech, written on the plane,
I've been told to say I'm *mezzo Napolitan.*
The line provokes an eruption of applause.
We trickle inside to where the banquet's set.
Over the boom of constant conversation
I can't understand, the band unremittingly plays.
Our plates are piled with enough food for three days.
The head of the Cultural Association
Is a leading jurist glowing with a cause,
A poet and painter of the avant-garde
Who networks with every particolored bard
And writhes on the dance floor like a teenager.
When I decline the olives and the wine
To the usual "What kind of Italian are you?"
The lady across the table puts me at ease,
Saying her husband is just like me, and he's

36

An Italian Italian. With her jewels and fur,
His dark brown suit, pink cheeks, and silver hair,
I assume he's a businessman indulging her
In the standard cultural eccentricities.
Later, I learn that he's a poet too.

2

Saturday. Frascati

The winds, cold even for December, come
Blowing across the belvedere, up from
The valley flecked with lights as far as Rome.
In the dingy upstairs auditorium
A woman in a big hat hands out fliers
Before the show, for the cultural enterprise
That she directs. My friend and I roll our eyes.
We know the type. Though the show is nominally
A poetry reading, on stage there's a company:
A drummer, some with saxophones and flutes,
And one at a microphone who whoops and hoots,
Whispers and bellows and grunts. He's not the poet.
The poet squawks through a trumpet, or his throat,
When something moves him. Not content to note
That life is meaningless, or simply state it,
They take about an hour to demonstrate it.
In a cantina on the edge of town
A professor of sociology from Milan

Invites me to join in the dancing, and I say
"*Sono americano, non ho un'anima.*"
Later, our hosts lead everybody down
To see the tunnels. As we form a ring
The percussion and the flute begin to play.
The woman in the hat proceeds to sing
Three troubadour *lais* in a voice so beautiful
That in the darkness all of us fall still.
I feel the stirrings of something like a soul.

3

Sunday. Rome

At sunset we emerge from Roma Termini,
My personal Virgil and I, and there they are,
Great swirls of birds against the purple sky,
Swerving and merging in an enormous blur,
Hurting the air with raw and raucous throats.
Because our bus is late, we stand in awe
At the spectacle and wax poetical
For one another's benefit. Not until
The Ritz Hotel engulfs us do we see
The spattered shoulders of our overcoats.
My friend's been rented by his publisher
To publicly present a brand-new thriller,
The first book of an investment manager.
He presents the furred and glittering audience

With clasped links of tradition and response.
The author in his turn starts in at once
To disavow all threads of influence,
Ingratiating with his ignorance.
He sells two hundred copies, while a RAI
Producer, the best-dressed man I've ever seen
Outside the pages of a magazine,
Threading the crowd to where my friend and I
Sit marveling at the spectacle, comes to inquire
If the book might make a movie for TV.
At the end, I shake the author's hand and say
"*Buona fortuna con il tuo romanzo,*"
Familiarly, no doubt superfluously.

4

Monday. Florence

Camera, backpack, sunglasses, a jacket
That says *The NFL on CBS*
And has a roll of film in every pocket:
The perfect American tourist. Who could guess
The thrill that runs through me like reverence
To stand in San Giovanni and to know
He stood here seven centuries ago?
Out in the sunlight, just across the square
The Duomo throws its shadow everywhere.
Whichever way I wander, I advance

Toward leather, diamonds, and the Renaissance,
Until I find the ancient town at last
Where even at noon dark alleyways wind past
Nine-hundred-year-old buildings whose ground floors
House souvenir shops and computer stores.
Do you seek his monument, traveler? Here are
Ristorante Beatrice and *Dante Bar*.
In front of the sand-colored house they say
He lived in (no one seems to know for sure)
I take my twenty snapshots and then pay
To go inside for the self-guided tour.
In a glass case little plastic knights portray
The battle of Campaldino. The entranceway
Has a giant poster tacked up on the wall
With the *Commedia* printed out in full.
But the version that they have for sale is small,
Its text is tiny and unreadable.

Serendipity

I know the word, of course. I always have,
And even where it comes from, Horace Walpole
And the three princes and the rest of it.
I've always loved it, loved to work it in
To any opening, apropos or no,
But just as with so many other words,
So many turns of phrase or turns of mind,
It took experience to make it mine.
The night before my last full day in Rome
I sat at dinner with an Australian scholar.
We talked about some poets of her country,
Hope, Kershaw, Slessor, especially McAulcy.
When I was young and even more contrary
I had enjoyed him only for Ern Malley,
Stripping pathetic emperors to the bone,
Wearing superiority as a cloak.
But now I liked him more as James McAuley,
A formal poet and more formal thinker,
A public paragon and secret sinner.
I'd met him often under other names,
At times I thought I'd glimpsed him in the mirror.
For my last day in Rome I'd planned a homage
To poets who'd never had the time to grow
A pack of selves to play off one another,
With visits to the house where Corazzini
Had come into the world and to the house

Where Keats had left it. But before all that
I meant to find my way to Trevi Fountain.
Deducting the three coins I planned to toss
And the costs of getting home, I had five euros
To fling as I saw fit. I'd planned my route,
I knew where I was headed, and I set off.
I'd walked for miles and all was going well
When all at once I found that I was lost.
I couldn't imagine how. It wasn't the usual
Making a mental note and then forgetting
Where I had left it. I had a map with me,
But I was lost. If you know Rome, you know
Whenever a *via* takes a turn of even
Eleven degrees, it's reason to rename it.
I thought that if I pushed on in the same
Direction I was going, I would come
Eventually to where I wished to be,
A plan that I'd pursued a thousand times
To everlasting rue. But I had a map.
Even so, I was compelled by chromosomes
To navigate without consulting it,
So I pushed on. In another block or two
I came to a small piazza where there stood
A bookstall. Hypnotized as usual,
I bent my head to scan the usual
Romances, monographs, biographies,
Hasty translations of American trash.
I'd looked at barely two or three squat shelves

Of paperbacks before I saw a slim
Gray hardcover crammed in, and on its spine
James McAuley * UNDER ALDEBARAN
—His first collection under his own name,
Published in Melbourne in 1946
In who knows how few copies. And I knew,
Even before I looked, that I would find,
When I opened the back cover, a pencilled "5-,"
And there it was. Amazingly enough,
I thought for a mad second I might put it
Right back where I had found it and keep looking.
A sworn contrarian, I knew I had
The entire book back home in his *Collected*.
For a second. Then I quietly surrendered.
Although it might not fit the definition
By professorial standards of precision,
Not even I would choose to be so uppity
As to refuse such perfect serendipity.

4

Truth

In memory of Joseph Dwyer

The good professor's letter on the desk,
The breath of human kindness in the lines,
The innocence of age and honesty:

The sentences smiled to him from the page,
Catching his eye as he was sitting down
To write a poem white with searing truth.

The old man's words sloped warmly on the page,
The sentiment lying undefended stirred
A momentary twinge in the young man

That he had pledged himself to writing truth,
Or that the truth he'd pledged himself to write
Could never be as nice as this old man,

Or else an instant of regret that he
Was not particularly nice himself.

From His Album

They knew I didn't want to go,
But they cawed from the car,
"Jemmy! Jemmy! Come on, you'll love it!"
They dragged me off to their picnic,
Plied me with their chatter
And sandwiches, even though
I sat all day in the crabbed corner
Of the field making faces,
Enjoyed themselves in spite of me
And spewed sunshine all day, even though
They knew I didn't want to go.

We sat in taverns and laughed,
Self-contained and overflowing,
Knowing. And everyone
Was a flaming poet in those days,
Doing great things. Now other beards
Brush the tables, all the great
Friends lean on one another's memories
On public benches, all of them
Spread-eagled on the rigging
Of days gone by, and no one knows
We sat in taverns and laughed.

The year she was thirty (could she have
Ever been thirty, or any other

Narrow age?), we danced all night
In the midsummer garden, where she
Pinned flowers on me, shook laughter
From the fold of her bosom, shook
Her laughter all over me
Until I would grin and caper,
Eager to play the harlequin
For her pleasure forever, or at least
The year she was thirty. Could she have ever?

Like Any Clown

The one who thinks he's in despair
Or nearly there
Crawlstrokes down the morning
Flapping translucent wings.

Beauty's withdrawn, tenderness,
The wet surrender
To the animals inside.
Bare wires partition the air.

Mouthing the slick bone
Of duty, he buttons buttons.
Windows, corners: everything has
Its essence, none of it his.

The hands do no good
For anything any more.
Nothing uses them any more,
Not woman, not wood.

Hiding in his life
He assumes a vertical posture
To probe the sockets of nature.
What jelly is left?

Once in a blue power
He bit into the flower
To unravel all the days. Expecting
Nothing now, he bites the flower.

The eyes are thicker,
Heavier all the time. They weigh the head
Down into the greatcoat.
He remembers the man who said,

You don't screw around,
You don't drink or dope,
If you're nuts it doesn't show,
So how the hell can you be a poet?

Imagination ravens to be old
On the back porch, all definition gone,
The pennants slack in a flat wind,
The work behind, forgotten, half undone.

Thirty years down, he wears
A smaller face,
Fills the minimum space,
Finds less and less to need.

Violins spiral from the stereo,
The window grows no bigger all the time,
The sun won't shine,
The rain won't let him go.

Beauty that shrivels with its sickly smile
Forgiving the stone world
Gets him nowhere now.
The beautiful is what survives.

Blunted with hope, he aims to stand
Hidden in the naked land.
His insides jump and dance like any clown,
He beats the line down to the possible.

Bombs shake the camera eye,
Shake the ground.
Pots rattle on the shelves,
The view holds steady.

The line holds steady. The sections of the brain
Click cleanly like a rifle mechanism.
Fingers crooking over the clicking keys,
Like any clown, he hits another note.

The Doorway

A poet cleans out his study, surrounded by
Shelves thick with slender books of poetry.
In the room below his wife is clearing breakfast.
His children challenge trees in the back yard.

His eyes skip lightly over rows of books
He hasn't read, whose elegant perfection
He still imagines, like the thrilling love
He dreams of making to his placid wife.

Five books piled on the desk oppress him over
The overdue review not yet begun.
He wishes the books were better than they are,
He wishes that we were better than we are.

Poking in the closet he finds a pack
Of songs he made at a woman years ago
Who scorched his nights so many years ago
With a love she called too pure to sink in earth.

Scoring their yellowed skin, the lines still smoke,
The thrusts, the towers pulled down on her head:
You led me out, you broke my head with love,
I scorn your silver flesh, your skimming soul.

No other demon will split my soul again,
I will be secret, suck on my lonely armor.
My bones I'll give them, with my bones I'll cut them,
But now I live forever for no one.

The clock taps out a quiet calculus
Of minutes from the wall. From the back yard
He hears his daughter's cry, his son's smart laugh.
He hears the vacuum's drone from the room below.

He lays the pages on the desk, across
New lines with fresh corrections written in:
Hide me in air, hide me inside your skin,
Hide me in the deep heart's dreaming core.

You Must Change Your Life

What would have been the price of another life,
Of Lisbon mornings, Alexandria nights,
Soiled cuffs in the office in the afternoon,
Grubbing in drawers, late suppers in candlelit
Cafes with unmopped floors, reading the smeared
Newspapers of a city left behind
By the dull progress of the meridian,
Freed from the pressure of significance,
Stumbling through angled alleys after midnight
With pauses for a long piss, a quick grope?

What would have been the reward of going home
To a spread of poems with cigarette-burn holes,
Cheese parings on the table, stains on the sheets,
A cardboard suitcase underneath the bed
With the few necessities, with all that matters
Carried inside the head, ready to go
At a moment's need, at the sharp knock on the door
That will never come, every day and night the same,
Bunched napkins with their hasty lines, a life
Squandered patiently in a city without trees?

Poets in Their Age

1

At the end of an afternoon
In early April, the air
Still laced with an edge of chill,
By the bookstore's poetry shelves
He turns, neat and precise,
Suit, topcoat, and briefcase,
Each silver hair in place,
To ask if my selections
Might find room for his *Collected*.
He shows me the book. I know
His name, and tell him so.
I recall his small success
Of thirty years ago,
Have heard that he is known
To be private and alone.
I'd be glad to buy. He quickens
At the recognition, sits
To inscribe his work, insists
On writing out in the back
Two newer poems, phrases
Burined into the book.
He hurries away. The door
Swings behind him lazily,
Letting evening in, as he
Walks into the falling dark.

2

Slow river outside the tall
Library glass in the warm
September sun. The small
Gently rumpled figure stands
At the podium that squeals
From the pressure of his hands
As he speaks of his dead son,
A man of my own age
Whose poetry I've admired,
Begging pardon again and again
For the sudden gasps of grief
That erupt as he tries to read.
At length he masters himself
To dispense the irony
And wit the age demands,
But as the pages pass,
As the images collect,
We hear the gathered pain,
We hear death in the lines,
And again the burble of death,
And everywhere the stark
Saying of death in poems
Written so long ago
In a proud prime, when to speak
The word was to conquer time.

5

The Ghost of Congress Street

Anne Longfellow Pierce
In her long whispering gown
Glides through her handsome house
In the heart of Portland town,
Over the flowered carpets,
Along the narrow halls,
Past nieces in gold frames
Smiling from the walls,
Up to the high windows
That looked down to the sea
When all the sky was open
And days moved gracefully.

A young and loving husband
Taken so long ago,
Her marriage a still moment
In the remorseless flow,
She came back home forever,
To gather a slow peace,
To tidy and to nourish,
To ease each one's release,
To thread the days together,
And most of all to be
Sister to the most famous
Man of the century.

Bread rises on the fire,
The gentle hours chime,
Laundry fills the boiler
As in grandfather's time,
The city rises higher,
Thick wires clot the sky,
But still the summer casements
Bring the seagulls' cry
To Anne Longfellow Pierce,
Who will not live to see
Henry's laurels nibbled
By the mice of history.

Anne Longfellow Pierce,
Licensed by City Hall
To live just as she chooses,
Uses the last of all
Portland's backyard privies
Till, when her time is done,
With all the calendars crying
Nineteen Hundred One,
She gives her body over,
She sets her spirit free
To fill the footworn hallways
In still serenity.

Light and Sweet

I saw you, Walt Whitman, childless, lonely old grubber...
—Allen Ginsberg

How Whitman would have loved it here,
This diner on this Sunday morning.

Clean with the chrism of the rain,
He'd track pure mud across the floor,

Fleeing the houseful of strange siblings,
The soldiers pleading from stained cots,

The Captain with his shattered skull—
All past his healing hands and heart.

What mouths he'd make at that mechanic,
Griefs he'd embrace in that old man.

What words he'd swap with the counterman,
Sturdy American sayings, bright with use.

Unbuttoned, hatless, large, he'd whoop
O counterman! O comprehensive nation!

Then we would cluster round him, stirred
By his wonder at the little jars

Standing at intervals along the counter,
Gathering and dispersing the salt of the earth.

Figures of Frost

Three fat books, each one thicker than his own,
Embalming every crack in the broad face,
Build testament to the monstrosity
Of genius, to the littleness of pride.

Admirers apoplectically provide
Long catalogues of generosity,
Glaze rueful smiles upon the weathered face,
Proclaim he fed on no flesh but his own.

An old man walks alone in a field of snow
So piercing white the sky's a smudge of gray.
His body slumps with the weight of all that's been
And the woven lines that hold the moments in.
He makes for the distant woods, so far away
No one can say how far he has to go.

Requiem for a Practical Possum

The grey fog tapping at the windowpane
Had come to spend the night.
The teacups tinkled on their saucers
For want of knowing
Anything else to do.
In the yellow lamplight
The old man's magic head
Tottered on the thin stretched neck
As he slipped into a fissure
(Be merciful to me O Lord)
In the cloud cushion that had just appeared
On the parlor rug.

The pages long behind him now,
Everything still within.
Brown river, rose garden at the root,
The rooms of solid women
(Let my cry come unto Thee),
Long evening walks
Through crooked Cambridge streets,
Dusk inking the stretched sky.
Past the blackboards and the brickyards
To the edge of the known world
Where the vast grey corrugated ocean called
With a human voice.

Stonetowered London, coldfingered rain,
The boneless multitudes unheeding
The smell of their damnation.
The daring clenched inside him,
The sudden cleaving,
The long letting go.
The firelicked shadows on the wall,
The scraping of taut nerves
(Wrapped in a burning sheet of sin)
And poetry, the strange
Images churned from a misery that changed
The taste of the air.

The bowlers, the umbrellas,
The barricade of books.
An owl's hard stare back into the camera
(And always there the one he had done in).
The podiums, the stadiums,
The arrangement of response.
A slightcornered smile as he stooped
To slide a flat hand over a flat book.
Arm linked in arm at last
And blinking eyes
In the sunlight, where a pair of ragged claws
Had become a rock.

The grey fog settled, wrapping the hour,
As the old man napping gently
By the fire (not the fire
That leaps to swallow up the lost)
Has done with his dry breathing.
Now he has climbed into that bower
He soiled tweed knees in sober search of,
Or he has fallen into that hole
He dreaded most,
Or worst of all
He has suddenly found himself to be a nothing.
He chose not to tell.

Uncommon Senses

A token for May Swenson

In the geographical
Center of a photo full
Of poets, a jumble
Of bards at festival
In their capital,
You stand stunningly small,
The white light at the core of all
The poems straining the cage
Of the page,
Making it squirm and bulge
With the surge
Of image upon image
Tumbling from the large
Longheaded sweep of your urge
To see, to touch, to get
Before things could evaporate,
Bubbling with the delight
Of how to take a cat
Apart and put
It back together not
Quite just like that,
The coffee always hot
And fresh, the roses wet
With real dew, every nuance

New once, and new once
More each time your mind invents
The call and response
Of each immense
And infinitesimal experience.
"Feel me to do right," you said
Your father whispered
On his deathbed,
Pointing you toward
What he had hid.
Now you are gone ahead,
Leaving us awed
In the land you illuminated,
Glad
To feel you, feel how right you did.

"Oh to Break Through"

It is too late
for any change
but death.
I am I.
　　—Robert Hayden

Dignified,
Unsatisfied,
His eyes caressed the world
He fought to see.
Born halfway blind,
Spinning his fate
From a many-selving spirit,
Turned from every corner,
How long must he wait?
It is too late.

He took the taunts,
Stared down the shouts
Of those who flaunted
Soul-shaped badges
In a holy zeal
To deride, to range
Through a world gone rotten
For the strident,
For the strange,
For any change.

Rooted nowhere
But in the soil
Of the one soul,
Walking the earth
With a stranger's name,
Fallen from his birth,
He turned whatever came
To hard beauty, and no force
Could freeze his mouth
But death.

The prizes and praise
They clamor to scatter
Over his memory
Fashion new ways
To obscurity.
Still it will not die,
Though sorrow's dust is spread,
The soft mouth
With its stubborn cry:
I am I.

Dark and Deeper

—I saw nobody coming, so I went instead.
                              —John Berryman

Sooner or later he had it all, the dry
And quiet hours, the leaping days, the halls
All full of heads turning to the one point
To see the one who was more so than themselves,
The sitting together with beer and smiles with those
Who were famous later and different, the nights
Of sweating it out inside the blasphemous dark.

Aging and deep and drunk, the spider's brother,
He flashed and plowed across the bodies of women
And wives to the number of three, who gave him feeds.
Let there be bigger houses. And there were.
In the middle still he sat, gray in his eyes,
Sucking the juice from cigarettes, but would dance,
Elbows and shoulders spindling in the sky.

Once was a clean and polite skull on the porch,
Then was a beard that flowed like power out,
Crackling with magic. Then was a day of ice.
Pictures in papers, and stories of the tank,
And no one whose help he would allow. A man.
To be is to be alone. What was a man
Is smashed bones in a hole, then will be nothing.

No hole for the little daughters, as no one hid
The ancient boy with the big and sorry father
Who looked to the water, but used a gun at last.
He grew and grew, till he walked out on the bridge
That he couldn't get across. On the other side,
From his public shames, he'd fashioned uprightness.
The skin was eaten. Nothing left to graft.

The books are solid, heavier in the hands
Than those of some who never miss the water.
With whips and chains he'd made the words stand up,
Proud songs and prayers to a Lord who never came,
Who came to be for a moment, to guide the arc
Of his long embrace to the earth. The words are black
And sharp, and forced forever from the white void.

Air of Lost Connections

(January 1988)

At forty-five
what next, what next?
At every corner
I meet my Father,
my age, still alive....
                        —Robert Lowell

Sky rich with bright blue emptiness,
The ice-glazed hillside gathers the hard sun
And flings the glare against the window glass.
The day is fresh. The times are fresh with styles
Your fevered dreams could not foresee.
You tilted at a flagrant enemy,
Now airy presidential smiles
Settle like stone. The empire pokes along.
My students with wind-burnished faces come
To be examined on your poetry.

Old flames, old puritans, old statues of
Your colonel stiff with virtue, freakish mercies,
The cold Maine mornings and the boiling nights,
The violence and the curdled love—
They write it out for me. What can they know
At twenty? Twenty years ago
In the still center of the days of rage,
To my smiling suave professor

(Now in his sixties, cored with cancer)
I called you "the Longfellow of our age."

You are clearer, ten years dead. From school to jail,
Family to fame, you walked from cell to cell.
The world was personal. You moved,
Married, talked to, lived with, loved
No one but writers. Nothing was real until
It was a poem, Hawthorne and Baudelaire
Truer than the flitting ghosts you saw
Around you. Impatient, awkward, inexact,
Your pen pricked facts. You strove to like yourself,
And saw a man too like yourself.

Heads down, my twenty students scribble,
Their faces knotted to unriddle
The life you wrote. The thighs inside their jeans
Straining with confidence, how do they understand
That we lose and are afraid? Behind the tired
Bewildered face, you lusted after honor,
Astride the bronze steed overmastering all.
You died in love. Amid the sprawl
The triumphs glow, the sad examples lean,
Stark milestones as we cross the frozen land.

Notes

"When in April"
Title: beginning of "The Prologue" to *The Canterbury Tales,* as translated by Nevill Coghill.

"A Suit of Sables"
Epigraph: *Hamlet,* III.ii.

"The Day"
"*I always made...*" and "*for it runs in my head...*": John Keats to Charles Brown, November 30, 1820.
"*The lungs were completely gone...*": Joseph Severn to Charles Brown, February 1821.

"Memorabilia"
The title alludes to Robert Browning's poem of the same name.

"The Choice"
Epigraph: "The Choice."

"The Free Man"
Epigraph: "In Memory of W. B. Yeats."

"*La Vita Letteraria*"
"*Roma campione...*": "Rome [soccer team] champion, Lazio [rival] balls."
"*Sono americano...*": "I'm American, I don't have a soul."
RAI: originally *Radio audizioni italiane,* now *Radiotelevisione italiana.*
"*Buona fortuna...*": "Good luck with your novel."

"Light and Sweet"
Epigraph: "A Supermarket in California."

"'Oh to Break Through'"
Title and epigraph: "The Tattooed Man."
I am indebted to P. K. Page's *Hologram* for the form of the poem, the Spanish *glosa*.

"Dark and Deeper"
Title: W. H. Auden, "The Wanderer."
Epigraph: "Henry's Confession" (Dream Song 76).

"Air of Lost Connections"
Title: Robert Lowell, "Memories of West Street and Lepke."
Epigraph: "Middle Age."

MICHAEL PALMA has published two poetry chapbooks, *The Egg Shape* (1972) and *Antibodies* (1997), and one previous full-length collection, *A Fortune in Gold* (2000), as well as *The Ghost of Congress Street: Selected Poems* (2008) online at theformalist.org. His poems have appeared in *Northeast, Pivot, Chelsea, Café Review, Rattapallax, Raintown Review,* and other periodicals, and several anthologies, including *Unsettling America, Wild Dreams, Sweet Lemons 2,* and *New Hungers for Old: One Hundred Years of Italian American Poetry* (Star Cloud Press).

His essays, reviews, and other prose pieces have appeared in *Chelsea, Shakespeare Newsletter, Italian Americana, Boston Book Review, The Journal of Italian Translation,* and *The Oxford Companion to Twentieth Century Poetry in English.* His essay "The Road to Rome, and Back Again" was reprinted in *The Pushcart Prize XXVII* (2003).

With Dana Gioia, he co-edited *New Italian Poets* (1991; named one of Ten Outstanding Translations of the year by the American Literary Translators Association). He assisted Ernest Menze in the translation of two volumes of the writings of Johann Gottfried Herder, *Selected Early Works, 1764-1767* (1992) and *On World History* (1997). With Alfredo de Palchi, he co-edited *The Metaphysical Streetcar Conductor: Sixty Poems of Luciano Erba* (1998). He is also the editor of the English-language edition of de Palchi's collection *Addictive Aversions* (1999).

His translations of many other Italian poems have appeared in journals, including *Paris Review, Grand Street,* and *Poetry,* and anthologies, including *Dialect Poetry of Southern Italy, Dialect Poetry of Northern & Central Italy, Via Terra, The Bread and the Rose,* and *Poets of the Italian Diaspora,* all edited by Luigi Bonaffini, as well as *The Faber Book of 20th-Century Italian Poetry* and *New European Poets.*

He has published translations of twelve modern and contemporary Italian poets: Guido Gozzano (*The Man I Pretend to Be,* 1981); Diego Valeri (*My Name on the Wind,* 1989); Sergio Corazzini (*Sunday Evening,* 1997); Armando Patti (*The Eye Inside the Wind,* 1999); Luigi Fontanella (*The Transparent Life and Other Poems,* 2000); Franco Buffoni (*The Shadow of Mount Rosa,* 2002); Paolo Valesio (*Every Afternoon Can Make the World Stand Still,* 2002); Maura Del Serra (*Infinite Present,* 2002; with Emanuel di Pasquale): Ljuba Merlina Bortolani (*The Siege,* 2002); Alfredo de Palchi (*Dates and Fevers of Anguish,* 2006; with Luigi Bonaffini); Enzo Carollo (*The Port and Other Poems,* 2008); and Maurizio Cucchi (*Jeanne d'Arc and Her Double,* 2011). His fully rhymed translation of Dante's *Inferno* was published by Norton in 2002 and reissued as a Norton Critical Edition in 2007.

For his translations, he has received the Italo Calvino Award from the Translation Center of Columbia University; the Raiziss/de Palchi Award from the Academy of American Poets; the Premio Speciale of the Associazione Culturale Campana of Latina, Italy; the Willis Barnstone Translation Prize; and the Raiziss/de Palchi Fellowship (for his forthcoming translation of Giovanni Raboni, *Every Third Thought*).

He has served three times as a grants panelist and three times as an expert evaluator for the National Endowment for the Arts, and has written several Teacher's and Reader's Guides for the NEA's Big Read program. A former Elector of the Poets' Corner at the Cathedral of St. John the Divine in New York, he is an associate editor of *Gradiva* and of *The Journal of Italian Translation,* and poetry editor of *Italian Americana.*

He was born in the Bronx in 1945. After many years of teaching, he now works as a freelance proofreader and editor. He has one son, Brian, and lives with his wife, Victoria, an occupational therapist, in Bellows Falls, Vermont.

CPSIA information can be obtained at www.ICGtesting.com
Printed in the USA
LVOW08s2202280214

375556LV00002B/507/P